children's
Letters
to
GOD

children's Letters to GOD

The New Collection

Compiled by Stuart Hample and Eric Marshall
Illustrated by Tom Bloom

Kyle Cathie Limited

Book design by Tom Starace
Illustrations by Tom Bloom
Cover design by Rebecca Foster

A CIP Catalogue record for this book is available from the British Library

First published in Great Britain in 1992 by
Kyle Cathie Limited
122 Arlington Road, London NW1 7HP
www.kylecathie.com

This edition published in 2009

Published in the United States by
Workman Publishing, New York

ISBN 978-1-85626-910-0

Printed in Singapore

10 9 8 7 6 5 4 3 2 1

Contents

The letters in this book express that part of a child's world reserved for special thoughts and wishes. The subject matter ranges through those beliefs, desires, questions and doubts that are urgent and common to all children. Some of the letters are disarmingly wise, others naive; some are knowing, some simple; some reverent, some not so reverent. Many are weighted with seriousness; others are lit with smiles. All of them are addressed to God with much hope and trust.

Grownups know for certain, of course, that the letters will not get there no matter how much postage they carry. But then grownups know so much more than children—sometimes.

In choosing these letters, we've tried to convey the incredible variety they represent. Their spelling and grammar have not been corrected, for what they say they say better as they are.

—*Eric Marshall and Stuart Hample*

Puzzlements, dilemmas and other imponderables

In Sunday School they told us what you do. Who does it when you are on holiday?

Jane

How did You KnoW You weReGod?

Charlehe

Dear God,

I read the bible. What does begat mean? Nobody will tell me.

Love,
Alison

Dear God,
On Holloween I am
going to wear a Devil's
costume, Is that
all right with you?

Marnie

Dear God.
Are you really invisible
or is that just a trick

Lucy

Dear God,
Is it true my father
Won't get in Heaven
if he uses his Bowling
Words in the house?
Anita

Dear God,

Did you mean for giraffe to look like that or was it an accident.

Norma

Dear God,
Instead of Letting people die
and haveing to Make new ones
why don't you just
Keep the ones you got now?

Jane

Dear God,
    Who draws the lines
    around the countries?,

        Nan

Dear God,

Do animals use you or is there somebody else for them?

Nancy

Dear God,

I went to this wedding and they kissed right in church.

Is that ok?

Neil

Dear God
Are there any
Patriarchs around
today?
                Patrick

Dear God
I like the Lords prayer best of all.
Did you have to write it a lot or
did you get it right the first time?
I have to write everything I ever
write over again.

Lois

God,
IT'S O.K. That you
made different
religions but
don't you get
mixed up some-times.

Arnold

Dear God
In bible times
did they really
talk that fancy?

Jennifer

Dear God,

I would like to know why all the things you said are in red?

Joanne

Dear God

What does it mean you
are a jealous God. I
thought you had everything

Jane

Dear God,

Is reverend Coe
a friend of yours,
or do you just
know him through
business?
Donny

Dear God,
Do you know about things
before their invented?

Charles

Did You Really Mean Do UNto Others As They Do UNTO You, Because If You Did Then I'm Going to Fix My Brother.

Darla

Dear God,
   When you made the first
man did he work as
good as we do now?
                    Tom

Dear God
My Grandpa says you were around when
he was a little boy. How far back
do you go?

Love
Dennis

Dear God,
I know all about where babies come from. I think. From inside mommies and daddies put them there.
Where are they before that? Do you have them in heaven? How do they get down here? Do you have to take care of them all first. Please answer all my questions. I always think of you.

Yours truly
Susan

Dear God,
I am English
what are you?
Robert

Fervent wishes, suggestions and complaints

Dear God,
Thank you for
the baby brother
but what I prayed
for was a puppy

Joyce

DeaR God
How come you didn't
invent any new animals
lately? We still have
Just all the old ones.

Johny

Dear God—

Please put another Holiday between Christmas and Easter. There is nothing good in there now.

Ginny

Dear God,
 It rained for are whole holiday and is my father mad! He said some things about you that people are not supposed To say, but I hope you will not hurt him anyway.

Your friend
But I am not going To Tell you who I am

Dear God

Why is Sunday School on Sunday? I thought it was suppose to be our day of rest.

Tom L.

Please Send me Pony
I never ask
for anything before
you Can Look it up

Bruce

Dear Mr. God

I wish you would not make it so easy for people to come apart. I had 3 stitches and a shot.

Janet

Dear God,

How come you did all those miracles in the old days and don't do any now?

Seymour

Dear -God- if-
we-come-back
as -something-
please-dont
let-me-be
Jennifer-Horton
because-I-hate
her.

Denise

Dear God,
If you give me
genie lamp like Alladin
I will give you anything
you want
except my money
or my chess set.
Raphael

Dear God,

My brother is a rat. You should give him a tail. Ha. ha.

Danny

Dear God,
Please send Dennis Clark

to a different camp
this year.

Peter

Dear God,
I wish that there wasn't
no such thing of sin.

I wish that there was
not no such thing
of war.

Tim M
age 9

Dear God

Maybe Cain and Abel would not kill each so much if they had their own rooms. It works with my brother

Larry

Dear God,
   I want to be just like my Daddy when I get big but not with so much hair all over.
                    Sam

Dear God,
    I keep waiting for Spring but
it never come yet. Don't
forget.
        Mark

Approvals,
confidences
and thanks

You don't have to
worry about me. I
always look both ways

Dean

Dear God,
I think the stapler
is one of your
greatest invention

Ruth M.

Dear God,
My name is Simon. Thats from the bible. I am eight and a half. We live across the street from the park. I have a dog name buster. I used to have a hamster but he got out and ran away. I am small for my age My hobbies are swimming, bowling, my chemistry set reading, coin collecting and tropical fish. Right now I have three kinds. Well I guess I said a Mouthful, Goodbye.

Always a friend
Simon

Dear God,
I think about
you sometimes even
when I'm not praying

Elliott

Dear God,
I bet it is
very hard.
for you to
love all of
every body in the
whole world
There are only
4 people in our
family and I
can never do it.

Nan

Dear God

Of all the people
Who work for
You I like
Peter and John
the best.

Rob

Dear God,

My brother told me about being born but it doesn't sound right.

Marsha

Dear God,

If you watch in Church on Sunday I will show you my new Shoes

Mickey D.

Dear God,

I like the story about
Chanuka the best of all
of them.
You really made up some
good ones.

Glenn

GOD,
I WOULD LIKE
TO Ø LIVE
900 YEARZ LIKE THE
GUY IN THE BIBLE
LOVE
CHRIS

Dear God
I love You.
how are You fine.
Im fine to
My Mother has five girls
and one Boy,
I am one of them.
Nancy 6

Dear God

I don't ever feel alone since I found out about you.

Nora

We read Thos. Edison
made light.
But in Sun. School THEY said
You did iT.
So I bet he stoled
your Idea.
Sincerly,
Donna

Dear God,

If you let The dinasor not exstinct we would not have a country.

You did the right thing.

Jonathan

Dear God. here's a poem

I Love You
Because you give
us what we need to live
But I wish you
would tell me why
you made it so
we have to die.

Daniel (age 8)

Dear God
It is great
the way
you always
get the
stars in
the right
places.

Jeff

God: the bad people laghed at noah— you make an ark on dry land you fool. But he was smart he stuck with you. thats what I would do.

Eddie

Dear God,
I do not think anybody
could be a better
God. Well I just
want you to know but
I am not just saying
that because you
are God. Charles

Dear God,

I didn't think orange went with purple until I saw the sunset you made on Tue. That was Cool.

EUGENE

Dear God,
I am doing
the best I can.

Frank